My heartfelt appreciation, gratitude, and thanks go out to my family and friends who encouraged, instructed, pressured, and gently shamed me into finally doing something with my poetry writing. Thank you for seeing the talent and gift in me—believing I had the means and the potential to get my writings in a book.

To my husband who looked at me like I had two heads when I told him I was writing a book—thank you for always being supportive of me in all my endeavors.

Thanks to my 3 boys who always cheered me on and were my audience as I rehearsed my poems.

To my Daddy Jesus—thank you for allowing me to finally get this book done. I am clear that I can do 'nothing' without your hand in it.

I would also like to take the time to thank Page Publishing for supporting me during this process. I am grateful.

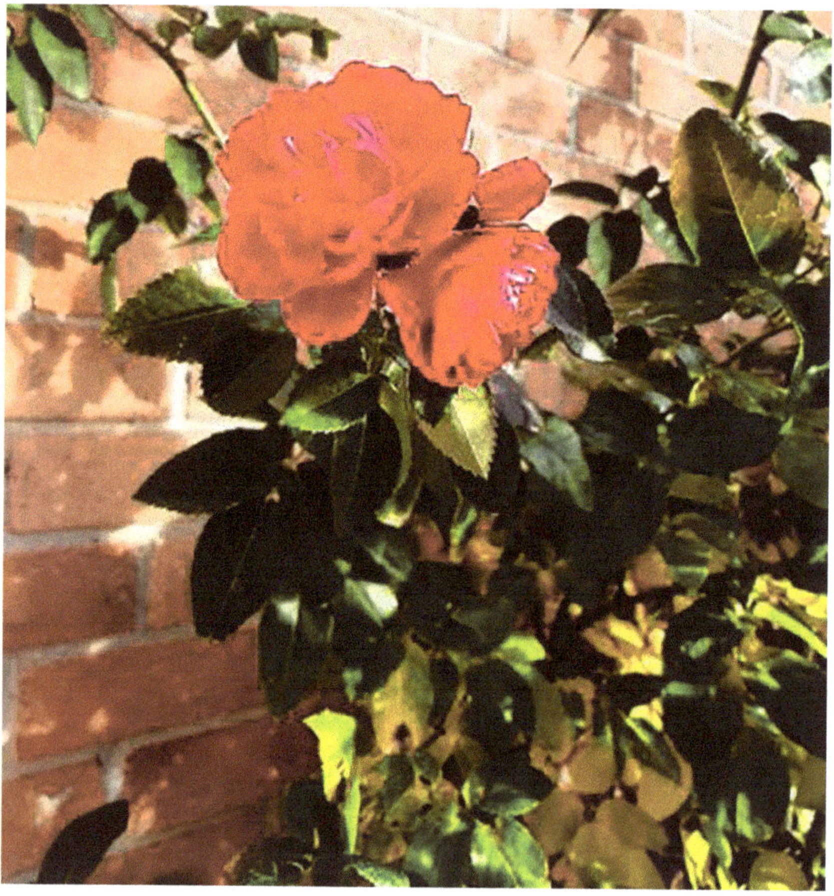

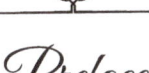

Preface

The good book says, "All scripture is given by inspiration of God, and is profitable for doctrine, for reproof, for correction, for instruction in righteousness."

Dare I say that these poetic rhythms and rhymes were also penned by the inspiration of God, for without Him, I can do nothing.

May you find a smile, an encouragement and some level of mental, emotional and spiritual motivation within these lines.

The View Point of Thankfulness and Gratitude

I live daily from the viewpoint of gratitude—not because everything is perfect but because through it all, I am still standing, and God made me smile again.

I have had my fair share of life's ups and downs.
I have cried in the night…and in the day.
I have lost.
I have had my fair share of surgeries.
I was told I would never have children—and should I become pregnant, the possibility of me bringing my pregnancy to term would be quite slim.
I have experienced heartaches.
I have experienced pain.

However, today…

I try my best to use every down as a step-up.
I use every up as wind beneath my wings to soar higher.
I don't believe any negative thing that is said about me.
I understand that good and not-so-good happen to everyone.
Girlfriend is still looking fine. (Yes, that's right.)
I have three beautiful, healthy boys
I have found faith and favor in the eyes of the Lord.

So yes…

I open my eyes everyday with thankfulness and gratitude because…
God has caused me to smile again.

Be Thankful

Be thankful at the start of a brand-new day
Even when you wake up wishing it would all go away

Be thankful for your breakfast delight
Even if there is no food in sight

Be thankful for your daily routine
Even if your boss and coworkers are mean

Be thankful if you have nowhere to go
You can pray for those who have to go

Be thankful for your family and your friends
Even when you wish the relationship would end

Be thankful for your vigor and strength
Even if you have failing health

Be thankful when everything is going right
Even when the way is dark as midnight

Be thankful at the end of the day
…And do not forget to always pray

Take my advice, do not think twice
Be thankful for all and you will please Christ!

In all things give thanks!

Amen!

Giving thanks always for all things unto God and the Father in the name of our Lord Jesus Christ. (Ephesians 5:20 KJV)

God's Extraordinary Grace

God's Grace is with us as we face each new day
And at the ending thereof...it does not go away

It abides at our side as we do our routine
With man's natural eyes it cannot be seen

Before you have your meal...they say, "Say your grace"
But the Grace of God surpasses food's taste

Parents often say, "God, give me grace before I 'bleep' this child"
But the Grace of God is gentle, patient and mild

It reaches down and pulls you from the darkest deep
And what we deserve we certainly don't reap

It protects your mind...keeps your body and soul
And cover those secrets that cannot be told

It gives you encouragement, brings peace and hope
The strength to go on...when you feel you can't cope

Whether you have it all right...or you're completely wrong
God's Extraordinary Grace gives you a chance to belong

His faithfulness is rich, everlasting and true
There is no discrimination in who you are or what you do

The resources of Grace...simply just cannot run out
Hallelujah for that, it's something I can't live without

I thank you Lord Jesus for your Mercy and Grace
Because of this favor, I'll see you face to face.

The grace of our Lord Jesus Christ be with your spirit. Amen. (Philemon 1:25 KJV)

The God of the Fireman's Hat

My son was around five years old. He needed a fireman's hat for a class presentation—just the hat. We searched everywhere—it could not be found. If we found anything, it would be the whole outfit, which we did not need (pre-Amazon/online shopping).

For those who have young children—or had young children—you can relate. Whatever the teacher said your child needed for a school play or presentation, you just had to find it.

One day while at work—stressing over where to find this fireman's hat—I got this strong impression in my spirit to go to No Frills and do some grocery shopping, on my lunch break. Of course, I tried to talk myself out of this. Who wants to grocery shop on their lunch break? Maybe a little retail shopping, but most certainly not grocery shopping. However, I could not shake the strong push to go grocery shopping.

So I went.

When I parked and exited my vehicle, I looked to my left and I noticed a little store that sold a variety of knickknacks. I thought to myself, "What a cute little store." I entered the store and directly in front of me, there it was, the fireman's hat.

God cares about everything having to do with *you*!

But my God shall supply all your need according to his riches in glory by Christ Jesus. (Philippians 4:19 KJV)

The God that Stopped the Wrong Plane To Get Us to the Right Place

So we were all set for our cruise out of Fort Lauderdale. The plan was to fly to Fort Lauderdale from Toronto, Canada, where we would hop on our cruise ship for a fantabulous one-week cruise. However, a day or two before leaving, we realized there was a miscommunication with our travel agent, and our flight was booked to Orlando instead of to Fort Lauderdale.

We were told, if we cancelled our flight, we would lose our money. So that was not an option.

After trying to figure out other options, it was decided that we would rent a vehicle once we arrived in Orlando, then drive to Fort Lauderdale, and hope beyond hope that there were no delays, that we did not miss any turns, that we didn't meet up on any traffic incidents because the slightest of delay would cause us to miss our cruise ship.

Needless to say, in the back of my mind, I knew we were going to miss the cruise ship. (Of course, I did not tell the rest of the family the disappointing reality.)

As lovely as I think I am, the cruise ship waits for nobody.

So there we were, waiting at Niagara Falls Airport, praying that this plane comes in on time and leaves on time. Praying for no delays because any form of hold up would change our complete family vacation.

Well, don't you know it. The plane was delayed and delayed and delayed.

I had to break it to my family that there was no way we could now, fly to Orlando, get the vehicle, and drive to Fort Lauderdale, and catch our cruise ship.

The plane was so delayed that it never came. Yes, you heard me right. The plane never came. It never showed up. 'Til this day, I was not given a reason why the plane didn't arrive in Niagara.

…But God…

As folks started approaching the counter to speak to the airline rep, we could see the sadness and disappointment on people's faces as they realized their vacation plans were ruined.

When I approached the counter, the rep asked me where do I want to go. I said to her, "Where I want to go and where I was booked in error to go is a different story." I explained to her our plans and the risk of missing our cruise ship.

The airline rep looked at me and again said, "Where do you want to go?"

It was at that point, I realized something bigger than me was happening. So I told the rep where we want to go. I said, "My family and I need to go to Fort Lauderdale—to catch a cruise ship."

All I can say is God stopped the plane from coming to Niagara Falls Airport because he knew the schedule we planned, we would definitely miss the cruise ship. So he stepped in and stopped the plane from coming, allowing us to get a flight to where we needed to go.

By now you can tell how this ended.

We were shuttled to another airport where arrangements were made to get us directly to Fort Lauderdale where we were greeted by our cruise ship and had a wonderful cruise vacation.

God stopped the wrong plane to get us to the right place.

The Lord shall preserve thy going out and thy coming in from this time forth, and even for evermore. (Psalms 121: 8 KJV)

DIVINELY POETIC | 7

The B-I-B-L-E
Part 1

The B-I-B-L-E
Yes! That's the book for me

From Genesis to Revelation
God's love story and inspiration

Whatever version you decide to read
Whether King James or the NKJV

NLT, Amplified, NASB
CSV or the JPB

What's the JPB, I thought you'd ask
Jamaican Patios Bible—sure fi bi a taahsk

Just open a version and you will see
God's perfect love given to you and me!

Man shall not live by bread alone, but by every word that proceedeth out of the mouth of God. (Matthew 4:4 KJV)

The B-I-B-L-E
Part 2

The B-I-B-L-E
Yes, that's the book for me

Words of Life, Words of Love
Freely given from our Lord Above

First John 4:7 to 21
Teaches God's Love—offered thru His Son

Commanding us to truly—love one another
Having perfect love for our sister and brother

To confess Jesus is God and dwell in Him
Our Lord and Savior—having His Spirit within

Knowing perfect love casteth out all fear
In times of certainty or when unclear

Reminding us to Love—those we see
In our differences and commonalities

So let's love each other in word and deed
For God is Love—in Perfect Beauty!

Far Above Rubies

Who can find a virtuous woman—the question is asked?
With wisdom, strength, and beauty—that's no easy task

Priceless they say, far above rubies, I'm told
This woman of honour, is a blessing to behold

Speak words so gently, yet work hard with her hands
Her exceptional quality is known throughout the land

The courage and tenacity to face each struggle in life
Puts a smile on her face, when words cut like a knife

Her poise and composure are a gift from above
Each difficult situation is dealt with love

The ability to make you smile through a tear
The scars of her life, she is willing to share

An Angel on earth, you can dare say
For in every situation, Christ leads her way

"I can find one," I loudly declare
And say it so proudly that all will hear…

You are far above rubies, not like any other
I'm blessed as your daughter… "I Love You, MY MOTHER!"

A gracious woman retaineth honour. (Proverbs 11:16 KJV)

To My Mommy
Thank you for the Ultimate Introduction

I lost my mother in 2005—however, her memories lives on!

Every year as we celebrate Mother's Day—I am once again in tears because you are no longer here with me.

I smile, however, when I remember how fussy you were about your appearance—your clothes, shoes, and hats.

You were so fussy about one thing and quite simple with others.

I remember when you introduced me to Kentucky Fried Chicken—you said that is all you wanted for your birthday, for Christmas and on Mother's Day.

Well, Mummy, Kentucky have changed over the years. However, the Ultimate Introduction you gave me still lives on…

The Introduction to Jesus Christ.

…and…guess what Mommy…?

…because of that Introduction…I will see you again.

Miss you Mommy!

Happy Mother's Day to the Women in My Life Part 1

To my Grandma:

I remember visiting you as a child—knowing you would have cookies and candies waiting for me to have my fill.

Grandma, you not only catered to my physical—Grandma, your hug was next to none.

Your hug had a voice. It said, "Safety, Support, and Love."

Now that I am grown and have my own children—with a level of

guilt—I have to admit, your sweet tooth heritage has carried on

…and

Guess what else Grandma? Your hug still speaks!

Love you Grandma!

Happy Mother's Day to the Women in My Life Part 2

Foster Mom:

I came to you unwrapped—a gift that was seemingly opened, torn, and put to the side.

However, you saw something in me and treated me just as one of your own wrapped gifts—making me feel alive and giving me purpose to do the same.

You fostered me and made me feel like a beautiful, wrapped gift. A gift wrapped in greatness.

Thank you Foster Mom.

Happy Mother's Day to the Women in My Life
Part 3

Single Mom:

You have been my mother and my father. You and I—together. Everything to me.

You single handedly carried, nourished, and protected me.

I was in need of nothing.

I often wondered how you did it—all alone? But as I grew older, I now understand—

you had someone holding your hand.

Today, I thank God for walking along side you—as you held me.

I appreciate you Mom.

Happy Mother's Day to the Women in My Life Part 4

The mothers who seemingly adopted me.

Thank you for standing in the gap…for stepping up to the plate and symbolically

feeding me when that was my need.

I appreciate you for giving me the gift of 'A Mother's Love.'

A reflection of God's Love for His children.

Such a beautiful experience I did not miss out on…because like Him—you gave me

You!

Thank You, adopted mom!

Father—an Expression of God's Love

Abba Father the Heavenly One
Created you in His image and called you son

And as an earthly token of His love to see
Out from your loins…He blessed you with me

My mortal shepherd, chosen for this role
Instill valuable treasures satisfying body and soul

Let me see in your eyes, unwavering assurance
Of your unconditional support through life circumstance

Build my character with wisdom and integrity
Live a life of example, it impacts my destiny

And when the abundance of your heart escapes your lips
Let them be words of life…my identity is built on this

With your arms of strength cover and let me know
You have laid your hands of blessings, over all I do and where I go

And as you busy yourself laboring and providing
My flesh may be full, but your quality time is more satisfying

Disappointments are inevitable, this we know
And our views may change the more I grow

Yet, a joy to your soul I always want to be
With your eyes full of expectation, whenever you look at me

Build a spiritual legacy—with Godly principles and hope
I'll need the foundation, when it's hard to cope

You're my mentor, hero, confidant, and friend
Desiring a relationship that will never end

And as your heavenly Father requires the same
I love you, my father, and proudly bear your name

Behold what manner of love the Father hath bestowed upon us, that we should be called the sons of God. (1 John 3:1 KJV)

A Prayer of Blessings on Your Dedication (For Baby) Part 1

Heavenly Father up above
Bless today this little bundle of love

Keep them safe and let them know
Your plan for their life—daily as they grow

Prolong their days in health and strength
Wisdom and understanding—rich in spiritual wealth

To the hearts of their parents—a joy to be
A credit to society, fulfilling their destiny

Unmerited favor, special gifts from above
Let them come to know you Jesus and your sacrifice of love

Today and forever in your presence continually
God bless and keep your precious child…
Love your friends and family!

A Prayer of Blessing on Your Baby's Dedication Part 2

As you are brought to be dedicated today
We offer thanksgiving and send a prayer your way

Requesting of our Dear Lord and Savior
To grant health and strength with unmerited favor

From the top of your head to the tip of your toe
Sustain body and mind, daily as your grow

A joy to your parents, may you always be
Being a credit to society, fulfilling your destiny

With a life of abundance, prosperity, and wealth
Knowledge and understanding, maintaining full strength

From this moment of innocence and until the years roll by
May you find your place in the Kingdom,
lifting God's name on high

Let your days be long, complete with wisdom and integrity
God bless and keep you always…We love you…your Family

Lo, children are an heritage of the Lord: and the fruit of the womb is his reward. (Psalm 127:3 KJV)

The Man Christ Jesus

Entered the world leaving His royalty and glory
Born of the Holy Ghost, what an amazing story!

Joseph, the name of His adopted Father
A virgin woman named Mary being His Mother

His purpose for coming was for you and me…
So we could partake in life eternally

Walked on this earth and dwelt among men
Like you and I, He had family, enemy, and friend

Living day to day fulfilling the Master's plan
From God to Jesus, then the Savior of man

Focusing daily on the business of His Father
There were days it seemed like He had no mother

A glimpse of His daily routine would be
Doctor, Lawyer, and Missionary

He invited Himself and walked in to your home
Didn't matter much if He had company or if He was alone

But when He left, your life would never be the same
That's one uninvited guest, you'd be glad He came

Encouraged the weak and lifted up the depressed
Open blinded eyes, and released the possessed

Emancipation! Liberation!—for every sin sick soul
The half of the story, they say have never been told

Healed the sick and raised the dead
Yet, negatives things about Him was said

Liar, alcoholic, and deceiver
Claiming to be 'God,' "He's a blasphemer"

The only one to stare perfection its face
Gave up His life for the human race

They couldn't take His life…remember He laid it down
Rose three days later…and put on His 'All Powerful' Crown

Hell can't touch Him for He has the key
The devil is defeated, power given to you and me

Risen today and now alive in us
My Lord, my Savior—THE MAN, CHRIST JESUS!

And the angel answered and said unto her, "The Holy Ghost shall come upon thee, and the power of the Highest shall overshadow thee; therefore, also that holy thing which shall be born of thee shall be called the Son of God." (Luke 1:35 KJV)

God's Redemption Plan
The Easter Story

Without hesitation, laid aside royalty and glory
The plan—to redeem man—and so began the Easter Story

"Behold a King is born" and given to earth
The majestic baby having a manger's birth

Emmanuel—God with us, Jesus—His name
To be the sacrifice for all, that's the reason He came

Building His Father's Kingdom—His routine would be
Healer, Deliverer, and Missionary

And at the age of thirty-three—in the fullness of time
Was brought to be crucified without committing a crime

To taste the bitter cup of death for humanity
So we could partake in life eternally

With a kiss of betrayal, Judas made the deal
…and for thirty pieces of silver—their fate was sealed

Crown of thorns on His head, feet fastened with nails
Enduring agony and pain, "King of the Jews" they railed

They pierced His side—blood and water flowed
At Calvary—His Love Amazingly showed

He hung on the cross—bearing mocking and shame
In omnipotent silence—He cast no blame

The Sovereign One—gave us His life that day
Fulfilling His prophecy—they couldn't take it away

Still powerful in death—for while three days in the ground
Took the keys of death and hell—destination—Heaven bound

Jesus rose from the grave, staring death in the face
Eternal Life now offered to the human race

From beginning to end, this was His Plan
Divinely orchestrated to redeem fallen man

Salvation now freely given to one and all
Embrace the Easter Story and heed Redemption's Call

For God so loved the world that He gave His only begotten Son, that whosoever believeth in him should not perish, but have everlasting life. (John 3:16 KJV)

Prayer—Kingdom Communication

Our Father sends the invite, "Come Boldly to My Throne
Enter in and Obtain Mercy, Where in Need, My Grace is Shown"

What a Glorious Invitation, What an Awesome Privilege
Having Access to God Almighty, the One who created us in His Image

To Communicate, a Dialogue…where the Father sometimes Speak
In the Stillness of the Moment…as His Face we truly Seek

His Attention is not Captured by the Eloquence of Speech
Oh…but His ear is eagerly Attentive when after Him, We Thirst and Reach

To Stand, to Kneel, to Fall before Him Prostrate
No specific posture requirement just Contrition and a Little bit of Faith

With a Heart of Humility, Brokenness, and Repentance
Requesting Wisdom, Knowledge, and Spiritual Guidance

Praying in Hope, Worship, Psalms, and Singing
Intercessory, Supplication, and Joyous Thanksgiving

Being Effectual, Righteous with Fervent Consistency
Fighting on our Knees—in Love—with Forceful Persistency

Entering Situations where our Feet may Never Touch
But the Spirit has No Boundaries…taking back…Such and Such

Interceding on the behalf of Our Dear Friends and Family
Remembering Thy Neighbor and the Needs of Thine Enemy

Trusting and Believing…that as We make Our Petition…
He'll send Healing, Deliverance, and Complete Restoration

For Our God is Sovereign…He Knows what is Best
At times—No Quick Resolve—it could only be a Test

Cry Aloud when in Battle…Yet knowing when to be Still
Releasing of our Desires…and taking Ahold of the Father's Will

For the Kingdom, Power, and Glory, Belongs to The Lord, so then…
Let's be Persistent in Prayer…In Jesus's Name…Amen!

Pray without ceasing. (1 Thessalonians 5:17 KJV)

Pray About Everything

So it was Saturday, August 28, 2021—we attended a wedding. After the wedding, we bought some food and went down to the lake to relax and chill.

Well, after chilling, our vehicle would not start. The engine wouldn't even turn a little.

I thought, "Well, my goodness. What was the point of that? After destressing by the lake, I am now stressed again." And so…my husband said that I should call our son to come and meet us with the other vehicle so he could boost it.

Well, every parent know that when their children just start learning to drive, whenever they are on the road, it is added stress for the parent. So the least amount of time they spend on the road, the less worried we are.

Correct?

I thought, "Why have him come all this way when we could ask someone?"

So we got out of the vehicle and I thought to myself, "God, you promised to hear us in everything. So right now, we need you."

So I asked my husband to open the hood and show me the part of the engine that turn when the vehicle starts. He said, "Hon, it is not going to start."

I said, "Just show me please."

He popped the hood, showed me where it was. I used one finger and touched the engine. I didn't say much. I just said, "In the name of Jesus, you will start and you will take us home."

My husband closed the hood. I asked for the keys. He said, "Hon, it won't start."

I went in, put the keys in the engine, turned it…and NOTHING!

My husband said, "Hon, it's okay. Let's call CAA because it is not going to start."

Before calling CAA, we asked a few people if they could give us a boost, which all had different reasons as to why they couldn't help us out.

I called CAA—they said they would come in twenty-five minutes.

I said to my husband, "Let's just go back to the lake until they come." He agreed.

However, just before walking to the lake, I looked up to the skies and I said, "Jesus, you promised never to let us down."

I said to my husband, "Try the vehicle again." I noticed this time, he was very quick to try again, we were on one accord.

I don't have to tell you what happened when he turned the keys…our vehicle purred and was ready to go.

Yes, Jesus hears everything and cares about everything that has to do with us.

Thank you, Jesus.

> **And Jesus looking upon them saith, With men it is impossible, but not with God: for with God all things are possible. (Mark 10:27 KJV)**

The Love Command

Shema!

Here, O Israel, The Lord Our God is One God.

One…

…as we should be…

The first command given to you…and me…

To love the Lord…who we cannot see…

Close to Thee

With all your heart, soul and mind…

The second command is of the same kind

…just like the first

In Matthew 22 and the 39 verse

To Love thy neighbor as thyself

Agape. Unconditional. Not situational

To Love…and have unity…between you and me

My brothers and sisters…beyond these walls…and

…Faith Sanctuary

> **Thou shalt love the Lord thy God with all thy heart, and with all thy soul, and with all thy mind. This is the first and great commandment. And the second is like unto it, thou shalt love thy neighbor as thyself. (Matthew 22:36–40 KJV)**

Sharpen the Sickle

Sharpen the sickle…get ready…
Sharpen the sickle…it's harvest time get ready…
My brother, my sister—take my hand
Join together, in Faith we stand…
Sharpen the sickle…

Sharpen the sickle…get ready…
Sharpen the sickle…it's building time get ready…
Progressing, growing, living in love
Fully connected—with the one above
Sharpen the sickle…

From east and west, north and south
This is what it's all about
Sharpen the sickle.

As iron-to-iron in Christ we grow
Building His kingdom down here below…
It's time to wake up, out of sleep
To spread the gospel, souls to reap

Sharpen the sickle…get ready…
Sharpen the sickle…it's harvest time get ready…
You've got yours and I've got mine
Sharpen your sickle, it's reaping time…
Sharpen the sickle…

Go ye therefore, and teach all nations, baptizing them in the name of the Father and of the Son, and the Holy Ghost. (Matthew 28:19)

Too Busy

Too busy to pick up the book God gave
Too busy to ask how His Son came to save

Too busy to find out why He died
Too busy to put the world aside

Too busy for church, too busy for Christ
Too busy to find out why He paid the price

Too busy to obey and live in His way
…you're even
Too busy to watch and pray

Too busy to save your dying soul
Too busy to enter into His fold

Too busy to ask about mansions on high
…but one day you won't be too busy to die

But seek ye first the kingdom of God and his righteousness and all these things shall be added unto you. (Matthew 6:33–34 KJV)

First John 4:7–21 (KJV)

Beloved, let us love one another: for love is of God; and
every one that loveth is born of God, and knoweth God.
He that loveth not knoweth not God; for God is love.
In this was manifested the love of God toward us,
because that God sent his only begotten Son into
the world, that we might live through him.
Herein is love, not that we loved God, but that he loved
us, and sent his Son to be the propitiation for our sins.
Beloved, if God so loved us, we ought also to love one another.
No man hath seen God at any time. If we love one another,
God dwelleth in us, and his love is perfected in us.
Hereby know we that we dwell in him, and he in
us, because he hath given us of his Spirit.
And we have seen and do testify that the Father
sent the Son to be the Savior of the world.
Whosoever shall confess that Jesus is the Son of
God, God dwelleth in him, and he in God.
And we have known and believed the love that
God hath to us. God is love; and he that dwelleth
in love dwelleth in God, and God in him.
Herein is our love made perfect, that we may have boldness in
the day of judgment: because as he is, so are we in this world.
There is no fear in love; but perfect love casteth out fear: because
fear hath torment. He that feareth is not made perfect in love.
We love him, because he first loved us.
If a man says, "I love God," and hateth his brother, he is
a liar: for he that loveth not his brother whom he hath
seen, how can he love God whom he hath not seen?
And this commandment have we from him, that
he who loveth God love his brother also.

How Much Do You Love Me?
Let Me Count the Ways

How much do You love me? Let me count the ways…
…of Your everlasting loving-kindness…this is not a passing phrase

For in Your omnipotent strength…before I was born…You knew me
and in Your omniscient power, looked ahead and saw what I would be

Like clay being molded in the hands of a skillful potter
You formed me in Your likeness…in the image of the master builder

Each member of my body, You assigned a specific role
Creating them for your praise, yet giving me complete control

And then the 'Breath of My Life,' in me You powerfully blew
Awoke Body, Mind, and Soul…Alive…just to worship You

…And to behold the world and the beauty thine hands made
The earth, the skies, and the mountains You laid

You even took the time to number the hairs on my head
Whether zero or over a zillion…that's what Your word said

At sunrise You present a bouquet of mercy and grace
To overcome my struggles and gain access to Your secret place

Where You restore my soul and lead me in the right way
With Your rod and Your staff offering comfort for each day

You promised to never leave…to be constant till the end
In time of joy or sorrow, You are a consistent friend

Whether I stand in absolute uprightness
Or be found—lost in complete sinfulness

You pull me closer and whisper so softly
"You are my child…I love you dearly"

Then to express love more greatly, You paid the ultimate price…
…and gave up Yourself as a living sacrifice

For no other reason, but to save mankind
Suffered on the cross…with me on Your mind

So how much do You love me? I just can't count the ways…
Because Your Love Is Everlasting…Oh Ancient of Days!

Who shall separate us from the love of God? (Romans 8:35 KJV)

The 2 Shall Become One

Opposites, yet inside an unrelenting attraction
Overwhelming thoughts, feelings of euphoria, capturing your entire attention

To be with, to talk to, to experience new things
What a blissful fascination? Listen to the heart sings

An outlet for your passion, one may say
To hold, to touch, discover in our own way

Hence, the ultimate occasion to vow before God and man
To live and love together, destiny, hand in hand

Facing the world with anticipation and pride
The bride, the groom, radiant—side by side

Abundance of dreams and expectations
He's mine, I'm his, adoration—sweet gratification

Then time escapes by, what has life offered since
In the world of marriage for the princess and the prince?

The romance, the freedom, the will to do
Until here comes baby, who's changing—me or you?

Sleepless nights, sometimes sickness and pain
Not to mention the in-laws, sent to drive you insane

You see my friend, it's orchestered in God's plan
In the marriage union—between woman and man

To face the inevitable of life, together not apart
Exhibiting endurance, solid, straight from the heart

Love, respect, and honesty
Unselfishness, gratitude, living responsibly

Combined to enhance one's married life
Offer freely to your partner—your husband—your wife

For when the pressures of life are all said and done
Then the miraculous union—The two shall become one

And the two will become one flesh.[a] So they are no longer two, but one flesh. (Mark 10:8 NIV)

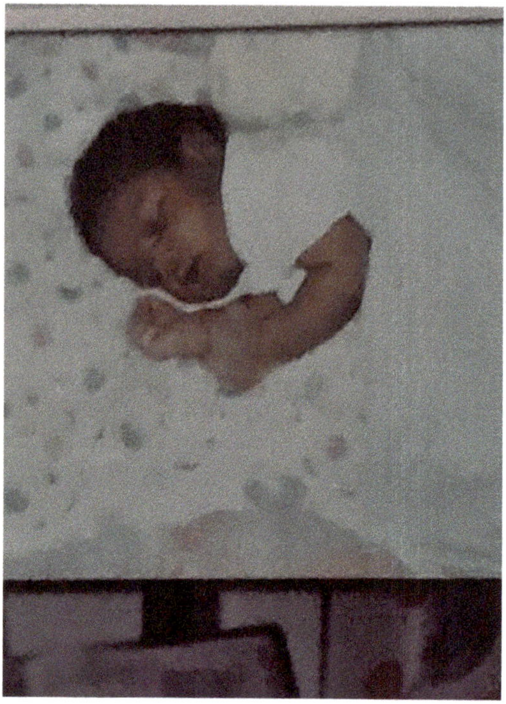

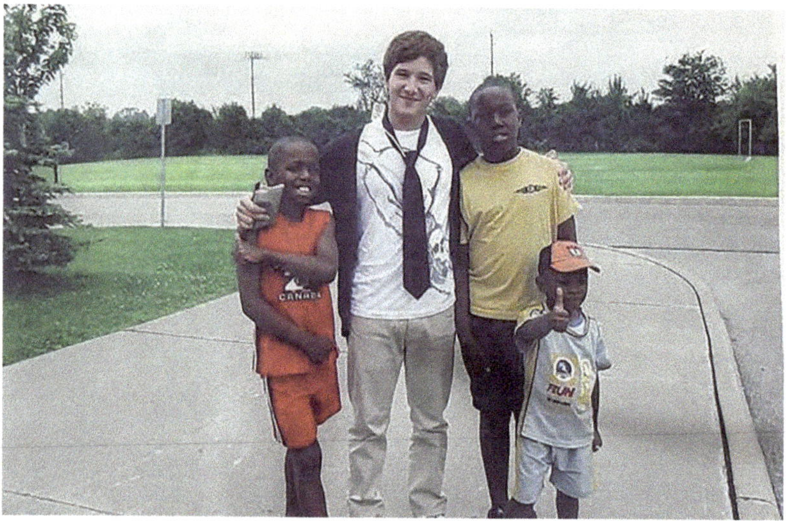

Wrapped or Unwrapped You Are Still My Child

Beautifully *wrapped*, You entered my world
Snuggled in my arms and innocently curled

…And although to Me…*unwrapped* You came
Still perfectly created and needing me the same

Your creation and existence are a part of the Master's plan
Wanting the best for you, He placed you in my hand

Knowing with your entrance…my life would change
Priorities…goals…focus…now all rearrange

You are a gift of love not given to all…
I'll instill positive counsel…guidance to stand tall

Endow you with love, nurture, and care…
Inspire, encourage—my knowledge of life to share

Yet as I give of myself and pour out of me
I must remember to replenish…you need me full, not empty

I'll find a place of renewal, restoration, and refreshing
Rejuvenate body and soul—spirit radiantly singing

For the rest of your life…of you I will be a part
May you see in my eyes, the melodies of my heart

For Wrapped or Unwrapped you've brightened my day
So take my hand in yours and let the Gift Giver lead the way!

For ye are all the children of God by faith in Christ Jesus'. (Galatians 3:26 KJV)

The Great Commission to Outreach

Before Jesus departed, the Great Commission He gave
Because the world He created needed to be saved

They have to hear…they need to be told
How He gave His life for both young and old

How He rose from dead and is still alive today
…and that for the Plan of Salvation…Jesus is the only way

Well, a thought…a suggestion…an inspiration…a plan
To leave our four walls and reach fallen man

But do I have the time for another commitment in my life?
I mean, I've got my own stuff, not to mention my family, children, my husband, my wife

And then how do we begin, how do we start
…It'll take a lot of sacrifice and a willing heart…

With a passion for the community…to encourage and teach
Ahh yes… "AliYaka…that's right, my son…we'll call it OUTREACH!"

With Preaching Points and Ministries sharing one ultimate goal
Laboring for the Master…to the saving of souls

Where Directors, Leaders, Team Captains, and More…
Do what we must…even Knocking Door to Door

We'll meet them in Prison…if that's what it takes
From the Streets to the Altar, all for the soul's sake

We'll have Deaf, Drama, Campus, and Bus Ministries
Vacation Bible School as well as Home Bible Studies

Serve Food to the Hungry…Visit the Homeless and Sick
Community Outreach with Barbecues or Picnic

Indoor/Outdoor Services and Church Evangelism
Extension Sunday School…just to learn more about Him

For the distressed, discouraged, those feeling they can't cope
Intercessory Prayers, Reconciliation Phone
Call, offering deliverance and hope

With Zeal and Dedication, a commitment to the Call
With Devotion and Loyalty, Kingdom Building, for His Glory, that's all

"Outreach" you are called, "Reaching Out" is what you do
May God Enlarge your Boarders and Bless Each and Every One of You!

Go ye therefore, and teach all nations, baptizing them in the name of the Father, and the Son and of the Holy Ghost. (Matthew 28:19 KJV)

The Cost of Freedom

The price for Freedom, the cost is high
The word starts with FREE…so I ask why?

Why the charge, expense…astronomical fee
To live…feel safe in my skin…free just being me?

Yet stories have been heard…stories have been told
Of the brave…the fearless…and the bold

*Rosa Parks, Harriet Tubman, Madame C.J. Walker
Wilson Rantus, Denmark Vassey, Martin Luther King Jr.*

*Sojourner Truth, Jesse Owens, Lorraine Hansberry
Malcolm X, Booker T. Washington…a long list of many*

They all fought for freedom for this present world
For every Man, Woman, Boy, and Girl

For respect, fairness, and equality
Without prejudice, discrimination, and partiality

But there's a hereafter…when this life is done
That's been bought and paid for by the 'Holy One'

See the King of all Kings paid for freedom from sin
Offering life eternal to all race, color, and skin

Free will for today…man paid the price…
Eternal, Spiritual Freedom, paid by Jesus Christ

Who gave himself a ransom for all, to be testified in due time. (1 Timothy 2:6 KJV)

Give Thanks It's Thanksgiving

Thanksgiving time is here again
To gather together with family and friend

Food in excess, decorate the table
Turkey center stage, eat as you are able

Yet as your lips savor the taste of gratification
Reflect on our world with heartfelt consideration

Where war and disaster some endlessly face
…And a daily dose of poverty…that's all others taste

Where Freedom is just another word
Of clean, running water…some never heard

The forsaken, the forgotten, those surviving without
Count your blessings my friend, that's what Thanksgiving is all about

Life may not be perfect…possessing all we need
Yet in so many ways…we are blessed indeed

So with Appreciation and Gratitude raise your voice and say
"Thanks for all my Blessings…this Thanksgiving Day!"

Let us come before his presence with thanksgiving, and make a joyful noise unto him with psalms. (Psalm 95:2 KJV)

For Unto Us a Child Is Born— For unto Us a Son Is Given

As it was prophesied so it shall be done!
The Virgin Mary shall bring forth a Son

Jesus—you shall call His name
'Emmanuel—God with Us'…the Angel proclaim

Wonderful, Counsellor, Prince of Peace
Everlasting Father whose wonders never cease

The purpose for His birth—to give up His life
To die for man's sins becoming the ultimate sacrifice

As it was prophesied so it was done
The Virgin Mary brought forth a Son!

In Bethlehem of Judea, He entered the world
Laying in a manger—Baby Jesus curled

And as He grew from boy into man
He never forgot His Father's plan

Touching people's life and changing their heart
"Come Follow Me" he said "Make a New Start"

As it was prophesied so it was done…
The Virgin Mary brought forth a Son!

On Calvary's cross became our Savior
Our Deliverer and Blessed Redeemer

Laid down His life taking on sin's shame
He knew His purpose—that's why He came

Three days later rose from the dead
Fulfilling every Prophecy as the Bible said…

As it was prophesied so it shall be done
The Virgin Mary shall bring forth a Son!

For Unto us a child is born, unto us a son is given. (Isaiah 9:6 KJV)

Desire to Inspire

One thing of the Lord we do Desire
It's to behold His beauty touch lives and Inspire

Inspire to change, Inspire to grow
Inspire to Share Jesus with everyone we know

To know of His glory and awesome splendor
Excellent greatness and magnificent power

Power to transform, Power to change
Power in a new walk…a life rearrange

With a Desire to Serve, A Desire to care
An expression of Christ, without favor or fear

To cheer, To Encourage, To spark a flame
And shine our light in Jesus' Name

To lift up the Fallen, to Strenghten the Weak
To dwell in His presence—after which we Seek

Desiring His Word as our daily bread
To be spiritually Inspired as His Word said

Committed to Excellence, Driven to Succeed
Laborers together—as Christ takes the lead

That others will Know and they will See
We Desire to Inspire at Faith Sanctuary

One thing have I desired of the Lord… (Psalm 27:4 KJV)

Life's Journey

As you journey through life, one thing is for sure
We will face difficulties, disappointments and hardship

However…

In the midst of the madness

We must keep an attitude of gratitude
Keep Smiling
Keep Positive
Keep Hopeful

I remember someone saying, 'The audacity of Hope.'

Yes, stare Hope in the Face and call it by name

Because as long as there is Life…there is Hope.

Hope

There is a Hope that is unshakeable and strong
A Blessed Assurance that gives a midnight song

Hope in discouragement, pain, and distress
It conquers fear, worry, and sadness

For past regrets, actions and mistakes
For wrong decisions and the choices we make

It gives you joy in time of sorrow
Calm and Contentment to face tomorrow

It quiets the soul in every situation
Gives a sense of peace without limitation

So where is this Hope…what does it cost?
It's in Christ Jesus—for the depressed and lost

It's a refreshing walk with Grace and Favor
Freely given, from our Lord and Savior

Today you can have it, just open up your heart
Put Your Hope in Jesus and make a brand-new start

Rejoicing in hope. (Romans 12:12 KJV)

As She Praised...

January 9, 2011—in the a.m. service—Faith Sanctuary
Praiser: Ceila Simpson
Song: Lord You Are Holy
As She Praised...something magnificent happened...
...Heaven cracked opened and allowed me to peek in and there it was...As she praised...

Heaven stood still...
The earth paused to listen...
Time took notice...
We rejoiced...
...As she praised...

The angels folded their wings and eavesdropped as her voice permeated the clouds.
Amazed as it were at the human instrument of praise
...As she praised...

Joy came...
Peace stepped in...
Divine unction was given...
We embraced the freedom and pleasure of salvation...
As she praised...

The Master's attention was captured...
His Spirit began to smile...
His ear danced to the glorious melody that tingled His lobe
He makes His presence known...
Oh, you should have been there...As She Praised.

Let everything that hath breath praise the Lord. (Psalm 150:6 KJV)

The Story of Noah

Once upon a time a story was told
About a man named Noah who was very old

When the sins of men came before God's face
Noah instead found favor and grace

So God told Noah about His plan
To flood the world and destroy all man

He then told Noah all he had to do
Was to build an ark and take in animals by two

For forty days and for forty nights
The rain outpoured killing all in sight

But Noah and his family they were saved
From the wrath of God and the watery grave

When the rain stopped and the earth was dry
God sent a Rainbow in the sky

It was a sign of the Promises God had made
Promises to Noah that will never fade

Genesis 6–9

The Proverb of Solomon

David had a son, they called him Solomon
He told a Proverb about Instruction and Wisdom

He said to be fair in all I say and do
Be kind to each other and make good choices too

If I listen to the wise and obey what they say
I will grow in wisdom each and every day

I should read my Bible—learn as much as I can
God will give me the mind to understand…

That I can live in this world and be set apart
If I honour the Lord with all my heart

Proverbs 1

Psalm 145 — I Will Praise You Lord

I will exalt you Lord, Our God and King
The Great Creator, master of everything

Your creation praise you—the flowers and the trees
The earth, the skies and the powerful seas

You take care of the sparrow and you take care of me
You alone are God, none other like thee

I will worship you Lord in songs and praise
And speak of your splendor—Ancient of Days

We praise your Glory and Your Wonder
Your Righteousness and Majestic Power

You are a good God—and you satisfy
When I'm discouraged, you hear my cry

I will bless you Lord and praise your name
You are eternal, yet you remain the same

You are the God of the Living…not of the dead
Having power over all, that's what your Word said

You are mighty and strong, you compare to no other
This generation praise you, Our Lord and Father

I will tell of your goodness and mercies to me
How you shed your blood to set me free

You are sweeter than candy, tastier than chocolate
Do you know Jesus—have you ever met?

He will make your heart glad and cleanse your soul
Change your mind and make you whole

I will let Your Praise become a habit of mine
To Bless You Lord Jesus—all of the time!

I will praise thee, O Lord, with my whole heart. (Psalm 9:1 KJV)

The Blessings of the Beatitudes

I'm Blessed, You're Blessed, We are Blessed
More than conquerors…enjoying God's rest

Jesus said, "Blessed are the poor in spirit for theirs is the kingdom of God"
With a humble heart heaven is mine and streets of gold my feet will trod

Jesus said, "Blessed are they that mourn, for they shall be comforted"
When tears of sorrows stain my face a sense of inner peace He sends instead

Jesus said, "Blessed are the meek, for they shall inherit the earth"
With lowliness of heart, we graciously become heirs to earth's worth

Jesus said, "Blessed are they who hunger and thirst
after righteousness, for they shall be filled"
If with earnest tenacity and passion I search for truth
He promised to satisfy for that's His will

Jesus said, "Blessed are the merciful, for they shall obtain mercy"
The act of kindness I release, in due season it will be returned to me

Jesus said, "Blessed are the pure in heart, for they shall see God"
To behold God's face maintain an upright heart that's one sure method

Jesus said, "Blessed are the peacemakers, for they
shall be called the children of God"
He'll call us His own—when with the preparation of peace our feet is shod

Jesus said, "Blessed are they who are persecuted for
righteousness' sake, for theirs is the kingdom of heaven"
When we endure trials for the cause of Christ the reward
reigning with Him forever and ever amen

Jesus said, "Blessed are ye when men shall revile you and persecute you and shall say all manner of evil against you falsely, for my sake"

When the words and actions of men wounds my soul for Christ's sake
I shall rejoice and be exceedingly glad for my reward
Will come on that Glorious Daybreak

The Beatitudes. (Matthew 5: 3–12 KJV)

We Are Blessed
(Part I)

I'm Blessed, You're Blessed, We're Blessed
More than conquerors…enjoying God's rest

Lost sinners we are saved by grace
Patiently running this glorious race

Living in this world, but not conform
Thru the Water, Spirit, and the Blood—we are now reborn

Knowing there's coming a blessed day
When Christ Jesus will come and take us away

Daily relying on God's Mercies and Grace
To bask in His Presence—face to face

Though mortal experience we must endure
Immortality awaits…that Hope is sure

That Hope we cherish, it is NOT in vain
Blessed Assurance—oh that Sweet Refrain

So whatever the trials, we must overcome the test
For we are more than conquerors, We Proclaim, We are Truly Blessed

Blessed is the man that trusteth in the Lord. (Jeremiah 17:7 KJV)

We Are Blessed Part II

Thru sickness and pain
Blessed
Sunshine and rain
Blessed

Job loss
Blessed
Testing your Faith Boss
Blessed

Relationship Struggles
Blessed
Sickness troubles
Blessed

Spouse doing great
Blessed
Still waiting for a date
Blessed

Children doing fine
Blessed
Want to disown them sometimes
Blessed

Got it all together
Blessed
Could be doing a lot better
Blessed

I'm Blessed, You're Blessed,
We are blessed
More than conquerors…enjoying God's rest

O taste and see that the Lord is good; blessed is the man that trusteth in him. (Psalm 34:8 KJV)

The Meaning of Christmas

C is for Christmas—that comes once a year
But Jesus is forgotten—and He's the reason it's here

H is how humbly—He came down to earth
The King came to mankind—through a Virgin's birth

R is for His Royalty—that He willingly laid down…
With His Majestic Power—and His Glorious Crown

I is for In Bethlehem of Judea—where He laid
Curled up in a manager—that's where His bed was made

S is for the Star—that was bright in the sky
Leading the wise men to Jesus—for Him to Glorify

T is for treasures—and the gifts they brought
To give and to worship—the baby Jesus they sought

M is for Mary—the mother Jesus chose
Also the one—to whom Joseph proposed

A is for As—you busy yourself this Season
Always remember—there is a Divine reason

S is for the Savior—we celebrate and say,
"Jesus—YOU ARE the reason—for every Christmas Day!"

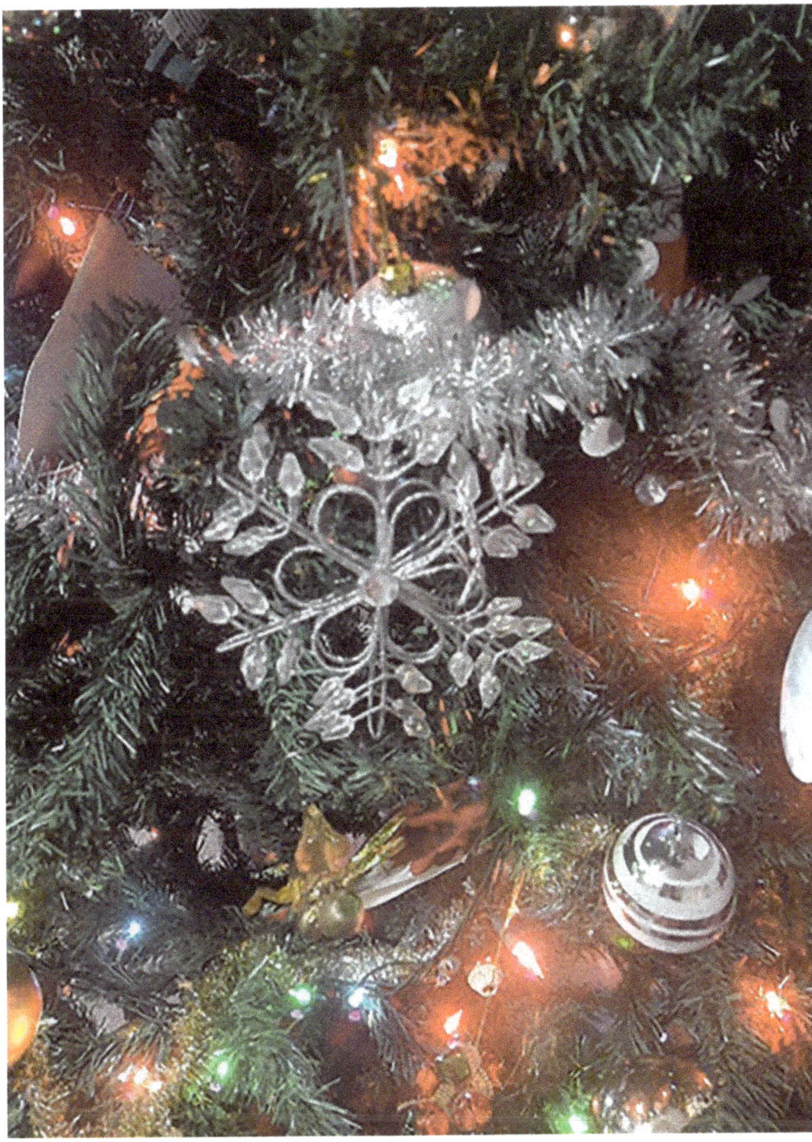

Faith Sanctuary Church Family

Mortal men we are, different nationality, background, culture, race
However, there are commonalities and vulnerabilities that we all naturally face

Desiring great health, finances, family, and friends
Peace and contentment…true love that never ends

Yes, we have differences, disagreements…our own proclivities
Opinions, mindset…personal frailties

Yet, on this one thing we all do certainly agree…
…that our world is bound by sin…needs to be set free

Believing God gave up His Son…the Lord Jesus Christ
Thru His death, burial, and resurrection paid sin's price

Therefore, in repentance, baptism, and being Holy Ghost fill
We accepted salvation…no longer 'Our Will'

Blood washed and cleansed…now the Redeemed
Brothers and Sisters…working for the Kingdom as a team

Laborers together sharing one common goal
Fulfilling the commission…sharing the gospel to every soul

No, we don't have it all right, and sometimes we just don't get along
But at the end of the day…we are all singing the same song.

Songs of Blessed Assurance and Amazing Grace
Power in the Blood to stay in the race

Songs of Eternal Life, Mansions, Streets of Gold
Heaven's Beauty…inconceivable…for to the ear, it's never been told

So whether you joined at Brownlea, Weston, or Jane Street
One body in Christ…till The Way Maker we meet

Depending on God's mercy…from day to day
…in Faith and Trust as He leads the way

Leader and Shepherd of this flock…Pastor Granville McKenzie
Brethren…united together…as…"Faith Sanctuary Church Family"

**Dedicated to my Pastor, mothers, fathers,
sisters, and brothers at Faith Sanctuary**

Family Day

Instituted by God from the beginning of time
As a reflection of His love and union divine

He made the first family unit known as Adam and Eve
One male…One female…don't be deceived

From that union came the human race
Variations, likenesses…from face to face

Each person relating to a specific Kin
By lineage, ancestry, bloodline…origin

A form of fellowship, a bond with some level of stability
A caring support system…sharing differences and commonalities

Touching each other's life in a significant way
Forming disposition and character by the things they do and say

Family builds the foundation for future development
To be a credit to society or to one's social detriment

As for the perfect family, we know there's no ideal
Disagreements, misunderstandings…hey, I'm just keeping it real

The treasure chest of family begins with Father and Mother
And could extend into priceless gems like sister and brother

Then there's uncle, aunt, cousin, nephew, and niece
Grandma and Grandpa, (family pet, Fido) the lists just never cease

Branches on your family tree may be many or just a few
Each one having some form of impact on you

So on the behalf of Faith Church Family, we open our Arms of Faith to you
Offering a Spiritual Relationship with priceless Brothers and Sisters too

A peculiar set of people—sharing eternal goals
Working for God's Kingdom to the saving of souls

Divinely connected by a purifying bloodline
You and I are the branches…Jesus Christ the True Vine

So today we honour Family, celebrating them for who they are
For the ones here with you and for others who are quite afar

We appreciate your presence and a prayer of love we send your way
That the Father Of All will Bless You on this Special Family Day!

Friend's Day

Today, April 25, Two Thousand and Ten
We extend a heartfelt welcome to you our visiting Friends

In spite of busy schedules, places to go and people to see
As well—there could be some other place you would much rather be

Yet you took the time to come and celebrate with us
As we acknowledge our Friends and Worship—The Lord Christ Jesus!

Be sure and know that He took notice too
That you placed Him first on your list of things to do

So in honour of you today and the Friendship we share…
Our bond, our connection, and the way you show you care…

…There is a Special Friend we'd like you to meet
Don't worry, just be yourself, He can be quite discreet

He's sincere and kind…having your best interest at heart
Maybe you already know Him or this could be a brand-new start

He's not hindered by culture, race or creed
Your background or history—His Love is guaranteed

Please don't turn away due to your secrets and fear
He knows all your secrets and as for fears…He's fully aware

He really takes more interest in being your True Friend
Offering unconditional love…without bias or pretend

Silver and gold we may not have to give
But we offer a priceless introduction to a Savior who lives

His name is Jesus…for you and I he died
Rose three days later…and today He is alive!

His friendship lasts a lifetime…then throughout eternity
Place your hand in His and fulfill your destiny

So today on Friend's Day we offer "A Friendship with Jesus" to you
Just have an open heart…and the rest He will do

"Thank You" for coming… "God Bless and come again"
Faith Sanctuary is glad to have you—our Dear Special Friend!

**Written when we had 'Family Day' at
Faith Sanctuary—April 25, 2010**

Access to the Man

Let us come therefore come boldly unto the throne of grace, that we may obtain mercy, and find grace to help in time of trouble.
—**Hebrews 4:16 (KJV)**

So:

- The God who said "Let there be light," and the light switch was turned on.
  You have access to Him!
- The God who spoke the world into existence
  You have access to Him!
- The God who created man from dirt.
  You have access to Him!
- The God who parted the Red Sea.
  You have access to Him!
- The God who told Joshua to march around Jericho till walls crumbled.
  You have access to Him!
- The God who stood in the fire with the three Hebrew boys.
  You have access to Him!
- The God who closed the lion's mouth and delivered Daniel.
  You have access to Him!
- The God who opened blinded eyes, healed the sick and raised the dead.
  You have access to Him!
- The God who put on flesh and called himself Jesus.
  You have access to Him!

So:

What do you need? Healing, deliverance, job, forgiveness, clarity, children, strength, direction, peace, hope, money, joy, love…

Go to Him!

Everything we need is in HIM!

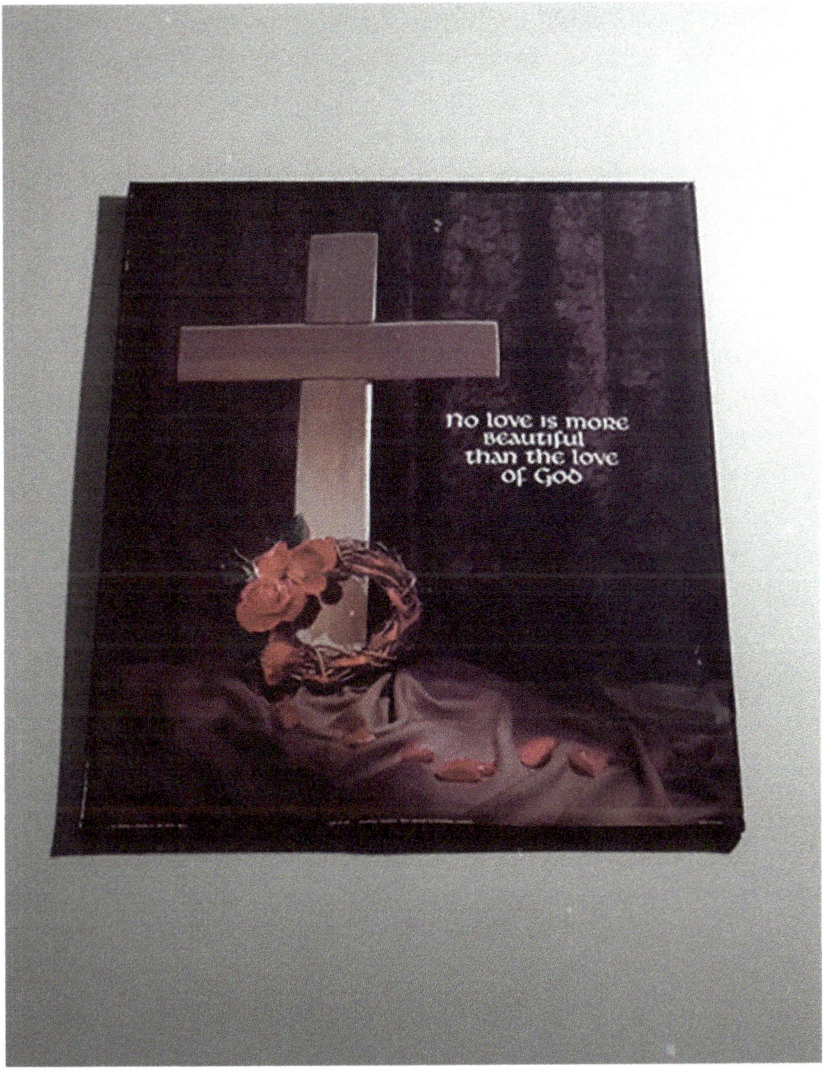
No love is more
beautiful
than the love
of God

Blinded for Our Good

> And as Jesus passed by, he saw a man which was blind from his birth. And his disciples asked him, saying, "Master, who did sin, this man, or his parents, that he was born blind?"
>
> Jesus answered, "Neither hath this man sinned, nor his parents: but that the works of God should be made manifest in him. I must work the works of him that sent me, while it is day: the night cometh, when no man can work. As long as I am in the world, I am the light of the world." When he had thus spoken, he spat on the ground, and made clay of the spittle, and he anointed the eyes of the blind man with the clay, and said unto him, "Go, wash in the pool of Siloam," (which is by interpretation, sent). He went his way therefore, and washed, and came seeing. The neighbours therefore, and they which before had seen him that he was blind, said, "Is not this he that sat and begged?" Some said, "This is he," others said, "He is like him," but he said, "I am he."
>
> —St. John 9:1–6 (KJV)

Just pause a moment and think about something that you have gone through in your life that was quite the mountain to conquer. However, after looking back over your shoulder, you have conquered it. Now if God had showed prior to that issue—what would face you—you would have thought for sure there is no way that you would overcome that trial.

Well in this story, the blind man was not able to see that Jesus was using his 'spit' to blend with dirt and put on his eyes in order for him to walk in his miracle and gain his sight.

Sometimes we are purposely blinded by God in order to bring us to the miracle—because if he should show us everything that is happening, we would say, "No, no, no. Don't put spit on my face, that is gross," or "No, no, no. Don't put my face in that situation," or "No, no, no. I can't do that." We would be crippled by fear, hesitation, doubt, and our own personal proclivities if God should show us everything.

So sometimes, God will purposely blind us until we are brought over to the other side of the miracle.

God's Got This

Judge not, that ye be not judged. For with what judgment ye judge, ye shall be judged: and with what measure ye mete, it shall be measured to you again.
—Matthew 7:1–2 (KJV)

Have you noticed that sometimes if you, your child, or someone in your family is going through a trial, testing, or struggle—your fault or not—there are folks who will add insult to injury and pass a comment, a remark, or treat you differently, slight you, shun you, and treat you as an outcast and make a statement predicting your finality.

All I say to you is, hang on just a little bit longer. If you are in the wrong, change, and just wait...

The tide does turn, and they are measured by their own judgement.

To My Church Folk

Please read 1 Corinthians 13.

God is not impressed with:

Our tongues
Our prophecy
Our degrees
Our knowledge and understanding
Our level of faith
Our giving to the poor
Our self-sacrifice—literally

…If we do not love our neighbor.

I Still Believe

Because I am one of those that don't broadcast my age…I will just say, ever since I was an embryo, I have always been in church.

I have failed many times. I failed people, family, myself, and God.

I don't understand a lot of things.

I have heard many things, seen many things—some, I wish I hadn't.

However…

After all these years, I still believe

Jesus is Lord

No weapon formed against me shall prosper

There is only one God

Faith Works

God is a deliverer

God is a healer

Jesus still saves

Jesus Loves Me!

I Still Believe!

Always Remember

God is always right.

When you are confused, he is not.

Treat others how you want to be treated.

Sometimes you may fail yourself.

God hears your faintest cry…he heard Jonah.

Life can get rough.

Sometimes you won't know what to do.

Friends will fail you.

Relationships will fail.

Children will drive you crazy.

You may get sick.

You may want to lose weight… (most common complaint) Lord, have mercy.

When you laugh, laugh loud and strong…for when you cry, it's loud and strong.

The madness can be real but just hang in there my friend. Take another bite out of life and chew it slowly!

Beautiful Bella Girl

Beautiful Bella Girl – that's who you are
Variety of shape, size, colour – as the midnight stars

Believe the beauty inside you – stand tall and take your place
Find beauty in character - not in the contours of your face

Empowered by the one - who holds the world in His hand
Embrace dignity, class and perseverance – do the best you can

Live life to the fullest – avoid discredit and shame
Where you can enter womanhood – having respect to your name

Love yourself from within – then let God's love shine through
Speak words seasoned with grace – favouring a pleasant attitude

Strive for excellence – achieve without compromise
Uphold self-respect, self-esteem – reach for the skies

Make a positive impact - during your time in this world
Believe, Empower, Love, Aspire - you - Beautiful, Bella Girl

X or Y Is the Variable

> **Every good gift and every perfect gift is from above, and cometh down from the Father of lights, with whom is no variableness, neither shadow of turning.**
> **—James 1:17 (KJV)**

Isn't it good to know that our God is not moody. No variableness. No changing. He does not wake up on the wrong side of the bed; he doesn't need his cup of coffee before we can have a conversation with him. (You know, you are like that or you have a friend like that.)

God does not treat us differently because of the color of our skin, hair texture, class, background, degrees on our wall, mistakes, mess ups, and mess downs. These variables do not change His love towards us.

As humans, we treat folks base on variables. However, in God, there is no variableness. He is the same yesterday, today, and forever.

With 'X' being anything you have done or acquired, God's Love + 'X' still = God's Love.

To My Young Brothers

Have your own stuff.

Buy your own stuff.

Don't have her buy it for you because you got her like that.

Don't mess with her mind.

Love her alone or leave her alone

Don't pick choose and refuse—hearts are easily broken and takes a while to mend

Stand like a man of honour.

Be the King of your Kingdom…and let them know it.

To My Lovely Young Ladies

Have your own stuff.

Buy your own stuff.

Don't rely on a partner for completeness.

Be happy—even when you are by yourself.

Smile often.

Don't be selfish, share a compliment.

Loneliness is horrible…but it is even worst
to have a partner and still be lonely.

Be the Queen of your Kingdom…and let them know it!

I Don't Know Why

I don't know why things don't always turn out the way we would like.

I don't know why most of us have a story that will bring tears.

I don't know why it's hard to find someone who you can trust completely.

I don't know why most women love shopping.

I don't know why men love to drive fast.

I don't know why the best tasting food are usually not good for you.

I don't know why we usually learn the lesson too late.

I don't know why money is spent faster than it is earned.

I don't know why people can't tell their REAL testimony.

I don't know why life gets hard at times.

I don't know why your best friend walked away.

I don't' know why love failed you.

I don't know why the grey hairs are coming in fast and furious

I don't know why the internet dropped at the best part of the movie.

I don't know why your last nylons were ripped by your nails.

I don't know why one piece of chocolate equals to ten pounds.

I don't know why mother's usually lie awake and fathers are out before you can count to five.

I don't know why men with big bellies are cute teddy bears, but for women it's much to bear.

I don't know why we are happy to find money, but hate losing it and never think about the person that lost it.

I don't know why the pen you grab for is usually out of ink.

I don't' know why children think they know it all.

I don't know why I can't resist chocolate.

I don't know why the rich get richer and the poor, poorer.

I don't know why the rabbit won't leave the vegetables in your garden.

I don't know why heartache is so painful.

I don't know why we have so much in common as humans and yet we are so different.

I don't know why they make the good food so expensive.

I don't know why there is always something to be had.

I don't know why we have fake eyelashes.

I don't know why it took me so long to write this book…

I just don't know!

I really want church folk to understand that lying is just as much of a sin as fornication.

Hating on your brother or sister is just as much of a sin as murder.

The consequences in man's eyes are different than God's. The eternal punishment is the same.

Remember—it's not the size of the sin that matters.

IT IS STILL A SIN TO STEAL A PIN!

Overcomers

The title of an Overcomer is a privilege to hold
For therein lies one's history, life experiences, stores to be told

Stories of success, failures, loss and gain
Triumph, discouragement, prevailing through pain

Midnight experiences - when it is hard to cope
Builds patience, longsuffering and blessed hope

This Hope is sure, it's alive and well
And that is why we are not ashamed to tell

That throughout life's journey we have come to know
God is in control daily strength He'll bestow

The Master Orchestrator knows what He wants us to be
So lessons must to be learnt from Life's University

Lessons of faith when direction is unclear
How to conquer those mountains when crippled with fear

We developed character, respect, virtue and integrity
Thru heartaches, mistrust, trials and difficulties

Through personal failures and our own inadequacy
We are patient with others extending grace and mercy

To become an overcomer takes endurance and strength
Not prominence nor distinction nor monetary wealth

We understand the importance of just being kind
Extending a hand – leaving no one behind

Outward may change, yet inward daily renewed
Living in favour and complete gratitude

We are resilient - more than conquerors
We are truly blessed – We are Overcomers!!

Who is he that overcometh the world, but he that believeth that Jesus is the Son of God? (1 John 5:5 KJV)

Ecclesiastes 9:11

The race is not given to the swift.

So it's not how fast you can run or how quickly you can get to the finish line, but easy does it. Mind your business, treat folks nicely, when it comes to people's struggles, have no comment.

If you mess up, get up, dust yourself off, step out from the mess, forgive yourself, and move on.

Know that folks may not always forgive you.

Take one moment at a time. One day at a time is too much; it may choke you.

Shine like the star you are in every situation. Trust your instinct. Have a godly mind and follow it.

Don't always trust your heart; it's quite emotional…

Get to the finish line by just putting one foot in front of the other, my friend. Godspeed.

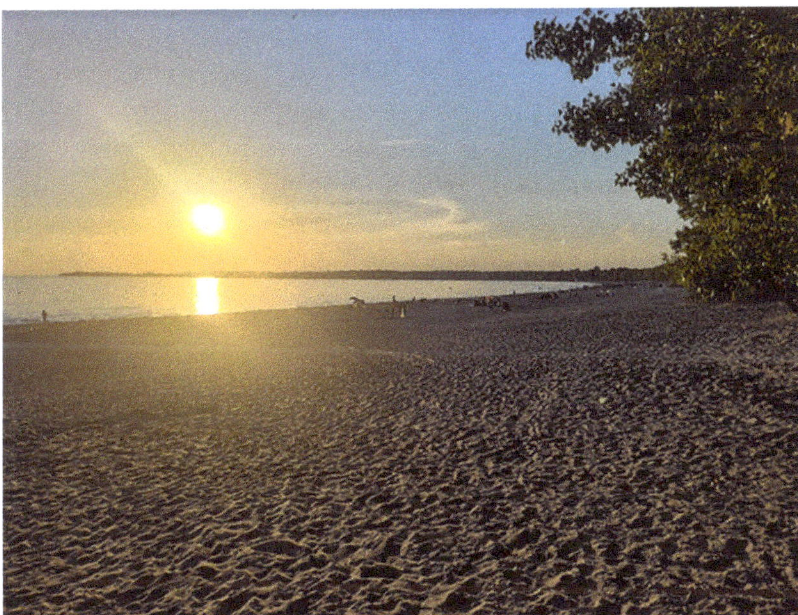

About the Author

Jean Clarke-Gillespie, also known as Jeanie Babie, Lady J, or Hon was born in Jamaica, West Indies, however grew up in Canada. She was brought up in the church and has been in church all of her life. However, she did not always allow Jesus to be in her.

She loves the beach, the sound of the waves, laughing, feeding folks and just seeing others happy. Her poetry writing started from when she was a little girl and continues to this day. Most of her poetry is presented in church, at birthday parties, baby christenings, and different functions. She continues to live every day in God's favor, faith, grace and mercies. Her goal is to remind everyone that:

You are priceless.
You are special.
There is only one of you in this big, magnificent world.
You are a child of God.
You are loved by God.
So go on with your beautiful self and spread the love of God to all!

CPSIA information can be obtained
at www.ICGtesting.com
Printed in the USA
JSHW041228250123
36775JS00004B/10

9 781662 451362